INVASION
on the
MOUNTAIN

Cover photographs by Richard A. Cofrancesco

Library of Congress Cataloging-in-Publication Data

ISBN 9781884592553

First edition, First printing

Published by Images from the Past, Inc.
www.imagesfromthepast.com
PO Box 137, Bennington VT 05201
Tordis Ilg Isselhardt, Publisher

Printed in the USA

Design and Production: Toelke Associates, Chatham NY

Printer: Versa Press, Inc., East Peoria, IL

BOOK ONE

THE ADVENTURES OF WILL RYAN AND
THE CIVILIAN CONSERVATION CORPS, 1933

INVASION
on the
MOUNTAIN

JUDITH EDWARDS

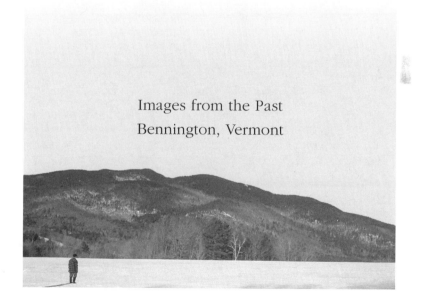

Images from the Past
Bennington, Vermont

To my own little corps
of mountain climbers —
my grandchildren

Contents

Will Ryan is peering out his farmhouse window on a late winter day in 1933. He's impatient for spring to arrive so he can once again spend his free time exploring "his" mountain, Ascutney. Will doesn't have much free time, though, with school and all the

chores his Uncle Em finds for him to do. Even worse, he finds out that his mountain is about to become the home of an entire army unit of young men and their leaders! How will the Civilian Conservation Corps and Will coexist on Ascutney, and what adventures will they share?

CHAPTER ONE

To the Mountain!

The steady drip, drip, drip outside his attic window brought Will to the surface. He poked his face up from the thick patchwork quilts, wrinkling his nose to gauge the temperature by how cold it felt. Hmmm. Not as cold as usual—and the drip. . . .

The ice must be melting! Spring, for sure! For sure! He heard his uncle bellow from the kitchen below. "Get up, you good for nothing. Cows can't wait all morning!"

"William, again! If I have to come up there you'll be sorry!" This from his Aunt Aggie. "I'm up, I'm up!" Will shouted. Already in his long flannel underwear, he pulled on his quilted flannel shirt and grabbed for his overalls, dance-stepping on the cold floor to locate his heavy woolen socks.

As Will hurtled down the stairs he thought, "Yes! Spring is for sure coming in. Time to go to the Mountain!"

The Mountain! His Mountain! Ever since Will's parents had deposited him on Aunt Aggie and Uncle Emmet's doorstep, never to be seen again, and long before he could much remember them, Ascutney had been his mountain. He could see it looming high above the land, three fields away. The Mountain was where he went to escape the drudgework that earned his "keep." Escape from Uncle Em's harsh rules and rageful temper. Escape from Aunt Aggie's whining, her genuine sadness which sometimes caused her to be gentle, but never warm.

Will Ryan knew every rock and crevice and winding turn up and down the huge stone mountain. "As-he-teek," one old Indian name. And it was his! Not today, not tomorrow, but soon, soon, the ice and snow would melt. Then he'd sprint across the fields in whatever time he could capture, and claim his world on Ascutney, the world where he belonged. The lush and delicate wild-flowers would greet him again, along paths made only by Will.

At the breakfast table he barely listened to Uncle Em's list of his laziness and how much Will owed him and Aunt Aggie. Loud, repetitive. Will was hungry because he knew what the day's chores were and they were hungry-making chores.

The other hunger, the one deep inside, was brought on by the melting snow. Pretty soon he'd be up there, on Ascutney, making his trails, feeling whole again.

Now, there was a worry. He needed to get his boots repaired for climbing the mountain—if they still fit him. At eleven years old, in early April of 1933, Will stood as tall as a medium-sized man, thin, wiry, and still growing. By the end of the summer those boots surely wouldn't fit, but he could start out with them. He'd take on more chores—sometimes his aunt and uncle let him sell eggs in town and keep the money, and sometimes he could take time to muck out a neighbor's barn—so he could earn enough to pay to get his boots fixed.

By midsummer, when all the snow had melted, he could climb the mountain barefoot, feeling every piece of moss and leaf and rock under his sturdy feet. In his mind he could see the trails up that mountain, a road to the top, campsites. He'd even be glad to share his mountain if people knew how wonderful it was and climbed it faithfully.

Enough dreaming, out to the barn to shovel it out and feed the cows. He couldn't stop thinking about the mountain, though. Will had learned that Ascutney had been tried before by some interesting folks. When he could get away to school he'd grab up any book that mentioned his mountain and talk with his teacher, who also loved Ascutney. First there were the Abenaki Indians. They called it "Ascutegnik," which meant "meeting of the waters." Some people thought it was originally called "Cas–cad-nack," which meant "peaked with steep sides." Both applied.

The Abenaki grew their corn on the rich Connecticut River soil, hunted in the woods, and caught fish in the river. Above them towered this rocky, luminescent mountain.

The Abenaki moved north before 1770 when the first settlers arrived in the Windsor area. They got busy building cabins and barns, and put horse and plow to Connecticut River soil, productive but never before turned over. Probably they hunted in the forests, used some of Ascutney's wood for building, and, who knows, took a day or two to climb way up to the rocky summit and see the whole Connecticut River valley from there.

And then General Lafayette was supposed to visit— "What are you doing in there? You think you're going to that schoolhouse today if those stalls aren't filled?" Guess who? Will sighed. But spring WOULD arrive.

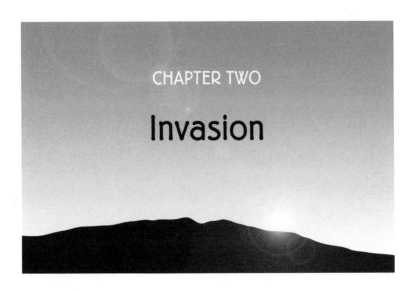

CHAPTER TWO

Invasion

One early spring day, Will drove the old tractor into town on an errand for Aunt Aggie. Coins in his pockets, he'd stop and get his boots repaired at the general store. Snow flowers were popping out, crocuses, tiny beginnings of daffodils, and Uncle Em was away trying to sell a cow.

The store handled pretty much everything—shoes, hardware, rope, tobacco, and food. It also provided news about anything important or unimportant, and today it was abuzz.

Will planned to wait while his boots were being repaired. No telling when he'd get back to town again. He paid John Davies, the storekeeper, and settled on a stool behind the wood stove; it was still chilly in the early mornings in late April. He let the customers' voices filter into his ears, which were so good at shutting out Em and Aggie.

The chatter was loud, excited, happy, annoyed, curious, and amazed—all at once.

"I heard they were going to start construction of barracks—barracks!—and a mess hall and a sort of officey-type building," said Ronnie Barlow, who worked at the blacksmith shop.

"Who is?" said Zeke Whitcomb, who was always asking questions anyway. "This Roosevelt fellow?"

"It was his idea, of course—he's the president!" snapped Ronnie. "Spending money he don't have while we can't even get dollar for dollar for our cows, all these give-away schemes. . . ."

The storekeeper stopped work on Will's boots, which made Will nervous, to chime in. "Now fellas, let's get our facts straight. There's been a lot of talk talk talk talk, here and all over Vermont, and what I can parse of it adds up to a darn good thing all the way around. Bunch of country and city kids with no work, families near starving, are going to get paid thirty dollars a month and send twenty-five home to their families. They're going to join this corps and fix up forests and mountains and roads and dams and all sorts of things—and yes, the government is paying for that."

"You mean it's like the army?" shouted Zeke.

"Well, the war fellows are handling it with rules and discipline but it's called the—"

"The Civilian Conservation Corps!" shouted another voice, belonging to Jamie Maken, who liked to read out things from the newspaper, as he banged in the door. "Listen to this! Unemployed, unmarried youth from the ages of eighteen to twenty-five, who have dependents and are willing to send most of the money back to their hometown and families, are going to be plucked up all over Vermont and the whole of the US of A and formed into these companies."

"What are they going to do?" Zeke asked in a puzzled voice.

"Build things. Dig things. Make dams and roads, and they're going to get educated too—some of 'em can't even read!" (A slight discomfort in the room.) "And they'll be here—in June!"

"Right here on Ascutney Mountain," finished John Davies, picking up a boot and giving it a big shake.

Will nearly jumped out of his seat. Ascutney? HIS Mountain?

"How many of them?" he burst out.

"Why, hello there, Will, didn't see you so quiet there. You want to join them and get Em off your back? Near big enough," said Jamie, who had witnessed Will's treatment at the farm and even tried to step in for him.

"Okay by me. These guys will bring business into town with what little money they have left after sending home," finished John Davies, handing Will his boots.

Everyone started talking at once, as Will tried to stop his brain from going pop, pop. . . . Maybe he could lie about his age and join up, maybe, maybe. . . . Well, he'd just have to go see for himself. He grabbed his boots and ran.

CHAPTER THREE

Sharing the Mountain

Loping across the fields after Sunday chores (just let Aggie try to catch him to go to church), Will finally headed for Ascutney Mountain. Patches of snow still covered the ground in shady spots. Three fields away he was at the base of the rocky, three-sided mountain. Ascutney stood alone in its wintry aspect, not a part of the Green Mountains that covered most of Vermont.

No hammering, no building; it was, after all, Sunday. However, he could see outlines of buildings in the field surrounding the base of the mountain.

Will wasn't the only boy who had climbed Ascutney. In earlier years groups worked on trails or went on

Sunday expeditions there. But now people just didn't seem to have the heart. Since the troubled money times in the Connecticut River valley, the trails had been allowed to crumble away. Will's teacher's father had been one of the men who formed an organization called the Ascutney Mountain Association, back in 1903. They went up the mountain to repair the damage from a fire in 1883 that had burned all summer long, according to Mr. Mansfield, Will's teacher. He liked Will a lot and encouraged him to keep up at school even though his attendance was spotty from Em's demands.

After the cleanup from the fire, the AMA went in to repair the Dudley trail—built in 1857 and named for the farmer who owned land there—and the Stone Hut on top of the mountain. This hut had been built that same year right on the spot, from stones cut on Ascutney itself! When they finished a big party was held, with seven hundred people attending. A band, a bonfire, hardy people piling in to spend the night at the Stone Hut. Will himself remembered a log cabin just below the 3,150-foot summit that he'd seen burn when he was eight years old.

Then Ascutney became Will's own mountain. It made life be okay. Out of breath, he stopped scrambling up snow-covered rocks to look down on the buildings about to take up the meadow below. Now, he would have to share his mountain. Well, he'd just make the best of it. As he climbed higher up he began to think, "Well, this just might be a real adventure."

CHAPTER FOUR

News and New Boots

The talk at the store, and with the few people stopping by the farm, was that 8,500 men each day had signed up for the Civilian Conservation Corps camps all around the country.

"Roosevelt wants these camps full-up by July! Give him that—he gets things done," shouted Jamie from his old car careening into the farmyard. "Hey Will, you done with those chores?"

"Never, Mr. Maken. Never!"

"Well, climb in, let's go down the store and jaw about this. I'll take the blame for kidnapping you! Let Em try to give me the strap! Leave the durn pitchfork, it's no good for my extra refined upholstery!"

Will had been up the mountain by his own special paths many times since he first saw the buildings going up, clearing, jumping, finding new growth, and even cultivating a little patch of snow flowers. The men who were building them weren't the young men of the corps, but some good construction people from around the state who were getting much-needed work. The buildings were progressing. By his birthday—May 20 when he would be 12 years old—he'd be ready to . . . well, ready to see what was what.

The boots were still a problem. He had grown way too fast already this spring and the boots were now too small. Em was in even worse moods these days, not feeling well and putting more and more work on Will. Em would not be inclined to put up money for a new pair of boots. Aggie was sad all the time; no use approaching her.

Jamie was gabbing away as he careened along, but he noticed Will moving his feet around uncomfortably in the too-tight boots. "Growed some, huh? You know, my old Pa really liked his boots—and honest, he didn't die in 'em. Just about your size! Course you're almost as big as me by now." Will knew that wasn't true, since

Jamie was about 6' 4" of all farmer muscle. "We'll just pull in here."

They landed in Jamie's farm, better tended than Em's and just cheerier. Before Will could protest Jamie pulled to a screeching halt and ran up the steps, yelling to his young wife, Jenny, who was setting some plants out on the porch. "Where are those boot collections of my dad's? Shh, don't say a word! I know he had a vanity about his boots."

Will nearly cried but he thought he'd just sit there. How he hated being a charity case!

Again he started hoping he could someway help the corps members with his knowledge of the mountain and feel good about what he knew. He guessed he knew quite a bit about Ascutney, come to think of it.

Jamie returned with two pairs of boots. And what boots they were. Hardly wore out, and one pair fit him perfectly and were much better than his old ones. Jamie insisted he take both pairs, just in case. He waved to his wife and off they went. Will was ready!

Camp under construction

Barracks

Camp buildings from above

Ready for dinn

Mess hall

CHAPTER FIVE

Will Makes Friends

W ill watched for a week as the camp was being set up. He was perched on a rocky ledge not far above the campsite—a quick hiding place if the busy men ever looked up.

First the men piled from the trucks and were handed packages. Then they lined up in front of a large, very official-looking man. "Okay!" he shouted. "Time for your shots."

Will cringed. Maybe he was just as glad he wasn't down there right now.

"Then go to your bunk room and find your cot, numbered. Fast!" Lots of scurrying around and emerging and re-emerging from the bunk room. Still dressed in their "civvies," the clothes they arrived in from home, the men were each handed a shovel and directed to a very large pile of coal and told to dig. Their destination was the trucks which would transport this coal to another camp. Some of the recruits worked as if they had a fire alongside their legs, and some got slower and slower as muscles, unaccustomed to such labor, began to tire. At 4 p.m. sharp they stopped. What would happen next?

Will knew he'd get a thrashing for not being home in time to do evening chores. So what? He'd stay here now anyway. It was summer, light would be good until almost 8 p.m.

Just after 4:30 the men reappeared in dress uniform. What a difference! Coal dust scrubbed off, ill-fitting, shabby clothes gone, the men looked like—men! He couldn't quite see them smiling but he bet they were. The men formed a long line called "retreat formation," Will found out later. At 4:45 sharp, the flag was lowered as they stood at attention. Oh, those uniforms! Will tried to picture himself in one, his gangly, bony, growing self, and nearly burst out laughing. One day!

The man who must have been the captain gave a small speech, saying civvies were no longer allowed except on the weekend day off, or they could go into town in their dress uniforms. Men would "fall out" each morning in denim work clothes.

As the men moved to the mess hall, Will tried to edge a little farther down the mountain so he could at least see in a window. Huge amounts of food on platters were being passed around, as the men sat on benches at long picnic tables.

The sight of all that food made Will hungry, though he knew Aggie wouldn't offer that kind of food ever and none at all for a while. He climbed back up a path that led him down a different side of the mountain. Wow! He'd be back tomorrow!

Will watched, whenever he could get away, for a week. He saw all kinds of things he didn't understand—but he did understand the tremendous work and discipline required of the young recruits. Their tasks were nothing more than what he did on the farm, but they were at them longer and harder. This was clearly a toughening-up experience for some of them.

He longed to talk with them, to make his presence known. Jamie had told him it was okay for people to climb around the mountain as long as they didn't go into the camp. How could he manage it?

Finally, after the first week, a group of corpsmen, feeling the heat, were loudly complaining that they needed to find some place to take a quick dip. Will knew just where they should look. So, he took a big gulp and left his perch and started down the mountain toward them.

"Hello! Who's this?" said a tall, very thin young man.

Will's heart was hammering. "Will Ryan, sir," he squeaked. His voice was changing and he simply couldn't rely on it.

"You from around here?" said the young man with a smile, taking pity on Will's nervousness.

"Yes, sir. I live on a farm three fields away. I come here a lot." He almost said, "and I love this mountain," as tears threatened. "I know a lot about Ascutney," and all in a rush added, "I understand you're looking to find water and I know right where you should look!"

"Ha! Spying on us up here? Well, show me." Three other men had gathered, looking no older and in two cases no bigger than Will himself.

"Say," said the youngest-looking one, "how come you're not in the corps?"

Will blushed and looked down. "Because I'm twelve years old."

"Holy mackerel!" Big laugh. "Makes me want to hit the food bag double! No problem with people climbing around on this mountain out of the camping area. So, lead on!"

Will started out at trot up the mountain. "Slow down, Will, I'm from Rhode Island. It's flat!" said the tall man. More laughter. Will slowed down a bit, but kept climbing.

The late June day was hot and humid, and the thought of a dip in a stream seemed good to everyone. "My name's George," the young man groaned, huffing and puffing along behind Will.

To the left they ascended by rocks that rose sharply upward. To the right the ground sloped sharply down the hillside toward the camp. They had come to a turn in the "almost path" where flowering plants cascaded down moss-covered walls of granite rock. From the center of this lovely picture a stream burst forth into a pool, inviting the viewer to jump right in.

"Holy Smoking Jehosaphat!" shouted a skinny blond boy the rest called "Alabama," as he did just that.

"This is the water I guess you folks are hankering to find. . . ." Will's voice was drowned out by three young men not exactly taking turns dipping into utterly pure mountain brook water.

"Hey, watch out, we're going to go back to camp soaking wet and get heck!" laughed George, shaking himself dry. "Hey, Will, you know any more special-useful things about this old mountain?"

"Oh, lots, sir, lots and lots," burst out Will, grinning over the gift he was able to offer.

"Come on, kid, come back to camp with us, we need a map. You can meet the big guys."

The little group arrived back at camp about 11 a.m., near the end of the morning work detail. Most of the corpsmen this morning were cutting down trees not needed around the camp, and splitting them into logs for winter firewood. Axes clanked, chips flew, and, in the rising summer heat, sweat glistened.

Will split wood all the time. Look at some of these sissies, he thought. City boys! Axes not swung high enough, so the blade didn't penetrate. Twice the work! He oughta show 'em. What he did instead was hang close to his new friends and listen to the voice of the foreman, who did know what he was doing.

George, clearly the spokesman for the group, approached the foreman and stood at attention. "Sir! Water-finding detail successful. Sir!"

Barking out one last order at a tired-looking recruit, the foreman turned to the group of three—plus one. "Successful, huh? You mean you found our water supply? Hope you didn't go swimming there—not allowed!"

Oh, my, what had they all done? Hoping they had all dried off, the corpsmen wondered who would be the first to lie! Will wanted to dig a hole and disappear into it.

"Well, thanks for warning me—official word will go out in announcements tonight." The foreman scowled, then almost doubled up laughing as he looked at their faces. He narrowed his eyes, still smiling. "Found a new recruit up there?"

Will turned beet red as the guys turned to him. Did they expect him to talk to this large, important stranger? Especially now that he had led these fellows up to a place he didn't know was the water source! That would be it—he'd never be allowed near the place again. "Uhhh," he started, then hurried on, "I know where other water sources are on the mountain—SIR—and I found 'em one nearby. I didn't know that . . ." His voice broke in the middle of a word. When, oh, when was he going to stop squeaking?

Taking pity on him, the blond kid from Alabama chimed in. "Kid's naught but twelve years old, if you can believe it. Climbs the hills like a mountain goat chased by a coyote! From around here."

"Hmm." The foreman actually smiled. "It's just about time to break for lunch clean-up. My name is Tom Olsen and I'm here to boss these guys into shape. And you are . . . ?"

"Will Ryan! SIR!"

"Okey dokey, Mr. Will Ryan. We'll have a little converse."

CHAPTER SIX

Advisor to the CCC

Will learned a lot in that "converse." He learned that the five barracks he'd seen under construction held fifty men each. He also learned that the major job for these young recruits was the building of a road up Ascutney Mountain. This road would be sturdy enough to carry car traffic up to a parking lot about half a mile below the summit, a place where many trailheads met. No road at all existed now, just rocks. Lots and lots of rocks.

The rocks would be dealt with by the CCC details, who would work with pickaxes, sledgehammers, shovels—and human sweat! Ledges and rock outcroppings would have to be blasted with dynamite. Already, gas-fueled compression jackhammers that would drill holes into the rock for dynamiting were on order. Once the rocks were less than boulder size (!) men with sledgehammers would break the rock up to make the roadbed. The recruits would use shovels and wheelbarrows to distribute the smaller rocks around the roadbed.

"I imagine that by the time these fellows get through with this road they'll be almost as strong as you are, Mr. Will Ryan." Tom Olsen smiled.

Will blushed again—darn bad habit of his that he intended to work on. But he liked the no-nonsense approach Mr. Tom Olsen took. Between him and Jamie mixed he could have had a real dad, something he'd never known.

"I'm supposing we invaded your special world, didn't we, son," Tom Olsen said, kindly.

"Er—uh—yes, sir." Will wouldn't blush, it was just plain true.

"Well, we can't make you a corps member—not yet—and I can't let you do dangerous things 'cause nobody's signed any papers on you for our boss, the government. Let's say, you can come over every so often and tell us things about the mountain we don't know, and be a kind of advisor. Eat some chow with us."

"Wow, really? That sounds real good—maybe better than being alone up here." Well, Will didn't really mean that yet, but he was looking forward to the months ahead in a way he'd never looked forward to anything before. But what about Em? He was already complaining, which meant yelling and hitting, about Will's being gone from the farm so much. A look of concern crossed his face.

"You in school, son?"

"Yes, sir, but not now it's summer. And no school any day my Uncle Em needs extra help, which is usually. I live at the farm."

"Orphan, huh?"

Blushing again. "Yes, sir, I guess you could say . . ."

"Me, too. Toughens you up." Tom Olsen grinned at the look of shock on Will's face. "We turn out okay, most times."

"Oh yes, sir, yes SIR!"

Olsen gave a big laugh. Will had made a friend. "Let's get some grub before those greedy youngsters get it all. Lunch is almost over and food goes fast around here."

That night, after a long yelling and swatting lecture from Em as to his whereabouts all day, Will settled into his bed, smiling all over. He'd do this, by golly, somehow. He wasn't trying to get out of chores, of doing his part. But to have his whole summer put on hold in case Em needed something, way past the already large amount of work Will did every day on the farm, just wasn't right. Maybe Jamie could help him out by talking to Em. . . . Then Will went to sleep and dreamed he was wielding a sledgehammer up on HIS mountain.

CHAPTER SEVEN

Rocks, Rocks, and More Rocks

T he date for starting to make small rocks out of big ones was early July, 1933. This was according to Alabama, whose real name was Percy, one of Will's special friends in the corps. George, who had introduced him to Tom Olsen, and Walter from Massachusetts who looked on Will as if he were the little brother he had left at home, were the others. None of the corps members seemed to mind his occasional presence and often asked him about the mountain.

By the end of June the camp routine was established. And what a routine it was! Will was used to rules, though the ones he had to follow were often made up at the last second by Em's anger. He was good at sensible things like keeping his room tidy and his few possessions out of the way. But Camp #129 of the Civilian Conservation Corps on Ascutney was the military!

Will learned that each man was paid thirty dollars a month; twenty-five of that amount was sent home to the man's family—greatly needed during what everyone in town called the "bad money time," officially the Great Depression. The families of the young men who had signed up for the corps were poor, struggling to feed themselves and, in most cases, to keep their farms intact. Jobs for boys getting out of high school or in the middle of it were almost nonexistent.

After sending money home, each corpsman had five dollars to use however he wanted—after laying out four dollars for a locker and using two dollars for a lock and hasp against occasional thieving.

On weekends the corpsmen could visit the villages of Windsor or Brownsville by walking or hitching a ride. They could go to the general store; John Davies was right when he had said this encampment would bring business to his store. In order to leave camp, the recruits would have to wear all civilian clothes, "civvies," or their complete uniform, including polished shoes. No mixing was allowed. "Serial number on all property." Walter had laughed, because it sounded just like the army.

"Our behavior will be predicated on the fact that we are all gentlemen and know the difference between decency and indecency," said one of the conduct rules in the long rule sheet. And if someone didn't know what that meant, they soon found out.

Will rushed through his morning chores and set out for the mountain almost every day, returning in time for evening chores except on the rare occasion when Em was away. Em had no other hired help. But no matter how much Will did in the early morning and evening, it was never enough. He was called on to do heavy-lifting jobs, much too taxing for a twelve-year-old, even with his strong frame. Em just piled on more.

Will knew that escaping to the mountain in August was going to be almost impossible. There were grain crops to get in, food crops to be harvested in readiness for Vermont's early winters, and late haying.

Even though Jamie was busy with his own farm, he came over several times a week to lend a hand so Will could "have a real summer," as he said to Em, not gently, one day.

"Em, nobody says a kid shouldn't do chores. But my kids are going to have some time to just do what they want in the summer, too. Life can't be all drudgery—soon enough for that."

"Well," growled Em, "he's not my kid. Didn't ask he be dumped here. He's just lucky I raised him up at all."

That was too much for Jamie, as he watched Will sweat and strain trying to jam together a split hay wagon wheel. He grew silent and turned away sharply, beginning to work something out in his mind.

Meanwhile, work had begun on the cascade of rocks running up and down Ascutney Mountain. Will watched the large equipment come in and was around at roll call when the road detail men were given their sledgehammers. He'd sure rather swing one of those than be putting together the old hay wagon.

A second detail was assigned to construct stone buildings and fireplaces, using rock from the large stones that were broken up for the road. A third detail would survey trails up the mountain, starting in about a year.

Will often imagined Ascutney Mountain as a great big earth-and-plant-covered rock—and he wasn't far wrong.

Hacking out a road from steep rock ledge was lots and lots of work! Progess was slow as trees were cut down on the road-site by men using bucksaws and crosscut saws. Jackhammers powered by gasoline-fueled compressors bored holes in solid rock, niches where dynamite would be placed in order to blast the rock apart.

Tractors found their way up the mountainside to move stumps and large sections of rock with winches and cables. Then the road crew got to work with their picks, shovels, and sledgehammers. They used wheelbarrows to carry and spread the smaller rocks and dirt to make a roadbed. Fill and gravel hauled in by trucks was spread on the surface to complete the road.

"I'll bet we'll have worked with at least one million yards of rock by the time this dingedy-dang road gets built," groaned Alabama as he threw down his sledgehammer to go to lunch. However, very few of the young men complained. Everyone was getting stronger and putting on needed weight because of the three big meals they were served every day.

Skinny and pale when he arrived at camp in May, Alabama was now tanned and sturdy. He still looked younger than the eighteen years that was the current lower cut-off age for a corpsman. One day, with a little time after lunch, Alabama came and sat by Will, who was himself enjoying an abundance of food whenever he was invited to "chow down."

"You goin' back to school in September?" Alabama inquired.

"Yes, I suppose so," sighed Will.

"Don't you like schooling?"

"I do like school. The teacher is good—we have a lot of grades together in one big room—and I like to read the things he gives me."

"Wish I could read," mumbled Alabama.

Will almost choked on his cobbler. "You can't read?"

"Nope. Quit school to help raise the little ones and sell wood when I was maybe ten. Didn't spend much time there before that, anyway. Now, I'm going to tell you a little secret—I lied about my age to get this job. I just turned sixteen last week. Ma couldn't send me a birthday card 'cause we didn't want to get found out. Makes a big difference to my family. But I always hankered to read. . . ."

Will thought a minute. Maybe Mr. Mansfield could loan him some books that were easy to read and then

. . . "Heck, Alabama, I could teach you to read. My teacher'll give me some books that you can start on, easy."

"I sort of know my letters," said Alabama, excitedly. "But you're just a squirt and when could we do it anyway? I know they're trying to get some folks in to educate us—lots of us can't read or not much, but it won't be for a couple of years. Think about it."

"You have Sundays off, maybe we could start some then."

Alabama looked embarrassed, and pleased, and hopeless, all at once. "Well, we'll think on it."

The duty bell rang, and Will ran up the road where he was showing the foreman a place on the rock where it would be easier to blast. He loved it when his knowledge of his mountain made him helpful so he wasn't just a little mascot, as George had kidded him once. But he'd think about Alabama and reading. Maybe Mr. Mansfield would be home today. If Will left the mountain soon enough he could stop by his teacher's house.

CHAPTER EIGHT

Reading, Lemonade, and Cookies

Will sprinted across the meadow to the little village of Brownsville. He'd never been to Mr. Mansfield's home before; he hoped it would be okay to stop by. People did that around here, but Will was shy. The little blue and white house was set up a flower-covered bank, with neat plants and flagstones around the front door. He didn't see a mudroom door, the porch entrance everyone went into around here, so he'd just have to knock on the front door.

A pretty woman in a dress and gingham apron answered the door. She held the hand of a little girl, also wearing a little gingham apron and holding a wooden spoon with icing on it in her other hand. "Yes, hello, can I help you?" the woman said with a smile.

"Uh, uh, I'm Will Ryan and Mr. Mansfield is my teacher in school and I wondered if I could talk to him about someone up in the bunch of men up on Ascutney Mountain." He stopped, out of breath.

"Well, of course you can. Come on in. Sally, go get your Daddy, he's out in the garden."

"I'm kind of dirty, ma'am, I've been up on the mountain."

"Oh, you're fine. If you like, we can just go through here and out into the garden to talk to Sam."

Sam! Will never thought of Mr. Mansfield as having a first name, never mind a pretty wife and a little daughter. Or living in such a clean little house with knickknacks and flowers and. . . .

"Why, hello, Will," said Sam Mansfield, as they met by the garden door. "What can I do for you? Here, come sit down. Connie, could you bring us some lemonade?"

Lemonade! "Oh, you don't have to bother, sir."

"No bother at all, Will—and I'm just about to put some cookies in the oven," said Mrs. Mansfield with another smile. Sally stayed, staring at Will and licking her wooden spoon.

Will told Sam Mansfield the whole story of his going up to Ascutney, helping out and getting sort of "adopted" by the corps, and about Alabama and how sad he looked when he said he couldn't read. He didn't tell him Alabama's secret—that he was only sixteen and had lied about that to join the corps.

"Well, I'd say that is the nicest story I've ever heard. And I'll bet you could teach him to read—you're the best reader in the whole school, did you know that?"

"Why, no sir, I mean, thank you, sir." Will was blushing again.

The lemonade and cookies were the best in the world, Will thought, and the plan his teacher came up with just might work. Until school began in the fall, and if Alabama was willing, they could meet at the schoolhouse at a certain time each Sunday. Each week the teacher would leave books and pencils and rulers and so on at a desk, and Will could leave a note after each meeting about what was needed next week. Will could have a key, if he didn't tell anybody—they both knew he'd be responsible for it. After school began they'd see what else they could do.

Full of cookies and compliments and plans, Will

realized that it was getting late and there would be holy creepers to pay if he didn't get home for chores. He began to look nervous and stammered that he'd better go, thank you so much.

"I understand, Will. I had a visit last week from a friend of yours, Jamie Maken."

"Jamie?" Will said, surprised.

"We're putting our heads together to see if we can come up with some way to change some things. Your Uncle Emmett isn't a bad man, just a rough and bitter one. Well, you'd better go, and you'll let me know what time Sunday is good?"

"Yes, sir, oh my, thank you!" Will left the garden by leaping over the hedge, which delighted Sally and her father, who picked her up. They both waved at a very happy Will disappearing fast across the meadow.

Jackhammer at work

Road building

Road in progress

More road
building

CHAPTER NINE

Practical Jokes and Chores

Not every moment at the CCC Co. #129, SP-1 (which stood for State Park Land) was hard work, rules, and meals! Will, who had grown up in a house with no brothers or sisters, a cranky aunt and uncle, and very little time to play, was often shocked at some of the practical jokes. He didn't even understand what they were—until George told him to climb into a bed he and a buddy had just made up. As Will tried to put his feet down into the bed, pulling the sheet up around him, he discovered that his feet didn't go all the way down the mattress. And it was all tucked in, just so! His look of shock as he realized that the top sheet had been doubled up to look like two delighted George and Walter.

"That's called short-sheeting. Standard greeting for new recruits, or anybody with a big head on his shoulders," George explained, laughing.

One of Will's schoolmates used to talk about putting toads in his little brother's bed or sticking chewing gum on the bottom of his boots; this seemed to be in the same league. Same kind of mean jokes, Will thought, but he laughed anyway.

Will learned about the goings-on in other camps, too, through George's letter-writing. George's family in Chicago had been so badly hit by the Depression that they had to sleep nine to a bed in winter to keep warm because they couldn't afford coal for heating. George had once gone to a private school, with small classes, and he loved to write. So any time he had free he wrote letters to corps members in other camps. He shared the replies with a few people in camp, and Will liked to be around when he did.

Once in a while Will pretended to go to bed very early after his evening chores, and then tiptoed out of the house and loped across the darkened fields to the mountain. He was welcome in the recreation center set up for the men on camp, as long as he didn't come in too often. One evening he got to the camp just as George had gathered a few people around him and was reading out one of the letters.

"Hey, Will, you have to hear this one! Now, don't anybody in this camp get any ideas—we'll be on to you. Evidently, upstate here, some guy with even more of an appetite than all of us figured out a way to eat more!" General squirming and laughter.

The rule was that, just like short-sheeting, "short stopping" was forbidden. Food came to each table in large pans or casseroles. Milk was in bottles and coffee in large pitchers. If anyone asked for a specific platter ("pass the pancakes"), the rule was to pass it non-stop—no interrupting the food on its way to the guy who had asked for it. Jabs with forks occurred when this rule was broken, and soon put an end to it.

"Well, this guy had a method. He would start to chew and then throw up! Then he would eat what he threw up!" Creepy, ugh, disgusting were remarks around George's chair.

"That was the point. Some guys just plain lost their appetites and left the table. So, this pig would get the serving dishes and shovel all the food he could into his mouth—wasn't sick a bit. He got away with this for a while by sitting at a different table every day. Took some time, but the men got onto him and would just look away and ignore him. End of that."

Will was aghast. He'd never thought like that, so sneaky. Other stories bothered him too. The worst one from another camp was about a fellow who bought a Mother's Day card for his mother, and put it into his locker so he could send it that weekend. He came back from working one day to find that the lock and hasp on his locker were broken, and the only thing missing was his card to his mother. The barracks leader tried to find the thief but couldn't; the letter writer said he had a suspicion but no proof. The very next weekend the man he'd suspected went "over the hill"—he deserted.

Will thought about that one. He had no memory of his own mother, and he wished he had a mother to send a card to. Then he thought about how much the thief must also have wanted his mother, enough to steal another man's card and then desert the camp. He was learning a lot more than how to break rocks!

The road continued to be built, sledgehammer blow by sledgehammer blow. Meanwhile, the detail

assigned to the stone buildings was beginning construction with rocks taken from the roadbed. Soon
there would be additions to the current buildings: the
barracks, the kitchen and a mess hall, the infirmary,
supply buildings, garages, blacksmith shop, recreation hall, boxing ring, officers' quarters, and the state
administration building.

One of the first of the original constructions had
been the small dam in Mountain Brook, north of the
Administration building—the dam rediscovered by Will
and his three CCC friends who had arrived after its
construction. There would soon be a stone picnic shel-
ter, at least a dozen fireplaces in picnic areas, and the
stone caretaker's house. When the road was finished,
a fire tower was to be constructed at the very top of
Ascutney, where none had been before. The stone
buildings would be made from Ascutney stone, along
with granite quarried from the old mines.

Will took in all of these plans and, as July faded into
August and he was needed more on the farm, he kept
them in his mind. He met with a suddenly shy Alabama
every Sunday at the schoolhouse. Mr. Mansfield had
put out the books and materials, and Will, after clear-

ing his throat, patiently went over the alphabet, the combinations of the letters to make words, and the beginners' books.

Alabama was so eager to learn, and so pleased with himself when he did, that by mid-August it looked as if he'd have the basics accomplished before Will's school started again.

Mid-August! Haying, more haying. Corn to be gotten in and canned, fence to be mended, wood to be cut and stacked before winter. And on and on. Down at the general store in Windsor, talk was about an early winter this year—maybe by late September. Was the government going to give subsidies for coal? Was the CCC camp, where so much wood had been cut, really going to come through with needed wood for the town? Windsor and all of West Windsor, which included Brownsville, was still mostly dairy farms. Prices for milk were low because people couldn't pay. Everyone worried as the Great Depression deepened. Farmers still had land and cows, but what if they couldn't sell their milk for prices that would maintain the herd for next year?

"Now I don't want to hear no bad talk about the boys at that camp," John Davies stated. "They come in here, all polite and dressed nice and spend their money. Let's me help you boys out by not having to charge too much just to keep my store open. And, we're going to have a road up there."

"Takes 'em a long time," said Zeke.

"So, would you like to be up there splitting those boulders?" scoffed John.

"No sirree, no sirree. I'll shut my yap!"

Will's Uncle Emmet slammed into the store, changing the mood as he often did.

"Looking for that good-for-nothing kid who lives on my farm," Em blasted out. "Disappears every Sunday afternoon with a whole pile of wood left to be stacked."

Zeke and a few others in the store were silent, and waved goodbye to John.

"Well, Emmet, seems Sunday afternoon in summer you maybe shouldn't work him so hard. Hey, you okay? You looked kind of pale just now."

"Mind your own business, about the kid and about how I look. Need a blade for a hacksaw."

"Okay, Emmet, okay." John got the blade he knew was the fit Em wanted and made a mental note to call up Jamie Maken on the party line, hoping not everyone in town would be listening in. Will was a good kid, and Jamie seemed to be cooking something up to get him out from under Em. But if Em was sick . . .

"Here it is, Emmet. Put it on your account? It's getting kind of big, you know."

"Put it on the account or don't sell it to me."

"Sure. Sure. Done. Good day to you."

John took advantage of the momentary lull in store traffic and called up Jamie.

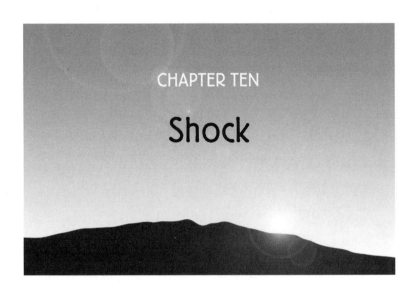

CHAPTER TEN

Shock

W ill arrived back at the farm late that hot Sunday afternoon, gloomily thinking about all the wood yet to be split and stacked. He didn't even go into the house. He just picked up the ax and started in. Stopping for a breather after a good pile had formed, he heard a strange sound. It sounded like a cow in distress, but it was higher, like a person. A person? He wiped the sweat on his forehead with his shirtsleeve and listened, moving where the sound got louder. It was coming from the house.

He ran to the back door and burst into the kitchen. Aggie was sitting on the kitchen floor, wailing. Wringing her hands and wailing. Spread out on the floor, arms outstretched, was Em. His face was purple and he wasn't moving.

"Aunt Aggie? Oh, oh." Will had seen dead animals many times, but right here in front of him was Em, his Uncle Em, who was mean and awful to Will and most everybody, but who was also what Will knew. What should he do? What would the foreman of the road crew, Tom Olsen, do right now? He was an orphan, and he had learned how to take charge.

"Aggie! Stop. I'm here. Stop." Aggie continued wailing. Will came up behind her and took her hands, holding her around the waist, this woman who had never thought to hold him. "Shh, shh. We need to get somebody. Come, sit down."

Little by little the hand-wringing and wailing stopped and Aggie, whimpering, let herself be helped up and led to a kitchen chair. Will knew he had to call for help—on the phone no one was allowed to use but was there, somewhere. Maybe he should check to see if Em was really dead, or just ill. But he just couldn't do that now. He'd get help.

The operator on the party line came on. Of course, now everyone in town would know, but then someone would come. "Hello, ma'am, this is Will Ryan out at Emmet Garfield's place. Ma'am, I think he's dead; could someone come?"

"Oh my Lord, Will," said the voice on the telephone. "I'll take care of that right away. This is Gladys. I'm used to emergencies, son, just take it easy."

Aggie had put her face between her hands and was weeping quietly. "Aunt Aggie, help is on the way." Will shyly put an arm around Aggie's shoulders, feeling awkward. A car door slammed in the driveway. Who could possibly have come over so soon?

There was a knock and Jamie Maken opened the kitchen door, his smile of greeting frozen as he took in the scene before him. "Oh, my golly! Well, I'll be tarnationed." He bent down by Em's purple face, picking up his hand and feeling the pulse. Aggie started to wail again and Jamie came over to Will, whose eyes were filling with tears.

"You hush now, Aggie, neighbors'll be by. Will, come over here."

Will found himself engulfed in Jamie's strong arms, and he let himself cry, silently, into Jamie's rough work shirt.

Jamie pulled him aside as his sobs subsided. "I'm sorry, Jamie, it's just so awful."

"Tell me what happened."

Will told him what he'd heard and seen, and how he'd spoken to Gladys to get help.

Jamie smiled. "Oh, yes, the party line is buzzing, I'm sure. She'll get the doctor and the ambulance and the sheriff here quick."

"How come you're here so soon?" Will said, relieved and not even embarrassed that he'd cried.

"John Davies, down at the store, called and said Em was there, nastier than usual, looking bleached-sheet white. Looking for you, loaded for trouble. I thought I'd better come out here and check. Looks like he got here before you."

"Is he dead?" Will asked, in a small voice.

"Oh yes, hope it was quick. Maybe Aggie'll know, but not the time to ask her."

Will had no fondness for this man who had no fondness for him, and who beat him down with words and sometimes with fists. But to see him lying there, gone, was a shock. This was the life he'd known— what would he do now?

As if Jamie had been reading Will's thoughts, he said, "There were some plans out there to get you away from Em's meanness way before today, Will. I was going to wait until end of haying to tell you, but when all the today stuff is over, you and me and Sam Mansfield—good man, even if he's not a farmer—are going to do some planning. Here come the troops—I can hear the cars now."

Jamie took Will's hand and, together, they opened the kitchen door.

CHAPTER ELEVEN

Incredible News

Word got out, somehow, to the CCC camp on Ascutney. Will had never complained about his treatment from Em and Aggie; he wasn't a complaining sort of person. But his clear discomfort when he was afraid he'd be late getting back to the farm pretty much told his good friends that he wasn't having an easy time of it. George, Walter, and Alabama were excused by foreman Tom Olsen from morning duty the next Wednesday. With him, they would pick up Will and Jamie and Sam Mansfield in a big truck and go on to Em's funeral.

Aggie had been "taken up" by a couple of neighbor women who had been worried about her for some time.

They had moved into the house to help her with her canning and regular housework, and their husbands helped out with the animals. Will kept working with them—cows on a dairy farm can't wait on funerals to be milked.

Will felt he should somehow be making Aggie feel better, even if she never had bothered about that with him. "Aggie's sadness is something people call melancholia, or a new word, depression. Only nobody knows, even here in 1933, what to do about it," Sam Mansfield told Will, as they waited for the CCC truck the day of the funeral. "It's partly that Em wasn't kind, but it's deeper than that. Maybe someday we'll understand why some people get sadness under control and some don't. But it isn't your responsibility, son. This is a community, and we'll figure out a way to help her out. Your Uncle Em sure never did."

The funeral was attended by most of the farmers around, though most of them were none too fond of Em, because funerals got attended. Will sat with Jamie Maken and Sam Mansfield and their wives. He sat next to Tom Olsen, who said one day he'd tell him about his Uncle Em . . . when he was older.

Where would he go now? Where would he live and what would he do? After the funeral, when the neighbor wives had served up the reception at the farm, he and Jamie went over to Sam Mansfield's house. Will found out about his future, right then.

"Well, Will," Jamie said, "Sam here and me—I mean your teacher, Mr. Mansfield—had already been pondering before Em up and died." Sam grinned. "I guess I could have put that better," added Jamie.

"You put it just right. Will, how would you like to come and live with me and Connie—and Sally? And you can spend lots of time with Jamie, helping him out but not slave labor like you did with Em."

Will was stunned. Live in that pretty little blue and white house with all those knickknacks? What if he knocked one of them over? He was terrified!

Jamie and Sam looked at each other, knowing how Will might take this.

"Will, you can also help out at the school, teach the younger ones. And, you'll have all the free time you want to go to Ascutney to keep those guys up there in line!"

Even Will smiled at that one. "What will happen to the farm? Who will take care of the cows and the wood and, well, everything? Where will Aggie go?"

"Aggie can't do it anymore. We're looking for a relative to take care of her. Meanwhile, the farm will be absorbed into the neighbors' farms—they'll rent fields and so on. You know, the property belongs to you—when you're old enough to manage it or sell it or whatever you like."

"That farm belongs to me?" Will was aghast. What did they mean by that?

"We've done some investigating through a lawyer friend of ours in town," said Sam. "Evidently the farm wasn't Em's to begin with—it belonged to Aggie's brother, your father. Em was just working it, because your dad had gone to college and taken a job as a geologist at a university. Your father and mother left you off at Em's and Aggie's because they were on their way to a wedding, for a weekend, at a friend's upstate. There was an accident and both of them were killed, outright. In their will you were deeded the farm. Somehow, that never got recognized. Certainly not by Em, who wasn't much nicer to Aggie than he was to you. Harsh reality for a twelve year old, but we'll help you through and it'll come out right in the end."

Will couldn't take in all of this, or almost any of it, right then. What he needed was to go up to the mountain, to climb and climb and climb. These were his friends. He'd just tell them the truth and they'd understand. "I have to run, to climb, to be on the mountain. Now. Thank you . . . do you know, uh . . . do you mind. . . ."

"Get out of here. Only not in those shoes." Jamie handed him his boots—the boots Jamie had given him in the first place. "Stay there as long as you want. Only come back. I'll be at your farm a couple of days—got some help at mine—and we'll figure it all out."

Will cried and grinned and grabbed the boots. Taking off his ill-fitting dressy shoes and socks, he said, "Okay, only I'm taking these and running barefoot. Thank you. Thank you." And once again he leaped over the hedge, only this time he headed for the mountain.

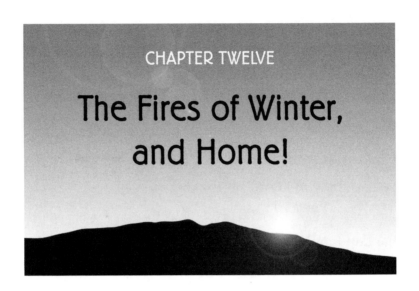

CHAPTER TWELVE

The Fires of Winter, and Home!

Winter came early to the Connecticut River valley this winter of 1933. Not that it didn't usually step whitely on the heels of autumn in Vermont.

"Wow," marveled Alabama, who had never before seen snow. "Lookit there—all that crystally white stuff just making its cold self right at home over those pretty fall colors on the mountain. And I get night watchman duty in December!"

Will had spent the fall getting used to sleeping in a real bedroom and looked forward to not having an icicle for a nose all winter. However, used to the rough but spacious kitchen and living area of Em and Aggie's house—now his house, which he still couldn't believe—he wasn't all that comfortable at first at the Mansfields'. As nice as they were, he still felt like a big bony mutt dog when he walked around their home.

Oh, but they were so nice, so undemanding, and they ignored his nonexistent table manners as he learned to imitate theirs. The best thing of all was little Sally, who adored him. He loved to play hide and seek with her, and to read her little books in the evenings. He went over to the farm to work some and helped out Jamie at his farm, and he loved school and still had plenty of time to lope off to the mountain.

The snow didn't make him happy. It was hard to get to Ascutney across the fields in winter, and it would get dark earlier and earlier. Jamie helped him make a pair of big snowshoes to cross the fields, which meant he could go over to the mountain at least some, all winter long.

Night watchman in winter! The big job was getting wood to stoke the barracks' stoves. Will's friends George and Alabama both had that duty, George in November and Alabama in December. The barracks were heated with big pot-bellied stoves and had to be kept going all night so the corpsmen could wake up to a warm room. All the camp buildings used wood for fuel. The wood the men were chopping the very first day Will met them had grown to a log pile weighing several hundred pounds. The top of the huge woodpile became covered with snow and ice, so a sort of cave, high enough for a man to walk into, had to be poked and pulled out of this mountain to get at the logs inside it. Otherwise frozen wood would have to be put on the fires, making for poor heat. There was always danger of the roof collapsing and dumping heavy logs on the person fetching the wood.

One late afternoon in mid-December, Will was at the camp, helping with reading along with the instructor, John Marshall, who had come in as educational advisor. Will's student that day was a gangly, awkward boy who had been almost too embarrassed to say he couldn't read. Alabama had told John Marshall that Will had started him out on learning to read. Since there were quite a few illiterate corpsmen and only one instructor, John welcomed Will's occasional help.

The temperature outside on this particular December day was almost too cold for snow to come down, but not quite cold enough. Snow started falling in blizzard proportions, and kept on, and on.

"Will Ryan," said John, "it isn't safe for you to go home through this. Go up to the captain and get permission to stay the night." There was a phone in the officers' barracks; someone would call the Mansfields and let them know Will was safe.

"This job is no picnic," said Alabama to Will, who asked if he could come along on Alabama's rounds. "It's a good deal though, because I get a weekend pass every other week and training as a firefighter. Also no KP duty. Hate potato peeling! The other watchman who's my partner, Jimmy Marco, and I alternate shifts on Friday and Saturday—midnight to 4 a.m., or 4 a.m. to 8 a.m. Tonight I have the midnight to 4 a.m. shift— maybe the snow will stop by then. We get up and have midnight chow, another good thing about this job. You're lucky this isn't the weekend! You game?"

Will was game! Alabama woke him at 11 p.m. Lights out was 9 p.m., so Will was distinctly groggy as he dressed and stumbled over to the mess hall with Alabama.

"Hot doggies!" exclaimed Alabama. "Look at that thermometer. It's 25 degrees below zero out there. No wonder my nose nearly froze off walking over here. At least the snow has stopped. You gotta get another jacket on if you're walking with me."

The first job was entering the "wood cave" and tugging the loose logs with a poker and tongs into a wheelbarrow. Then the load was wheeled to each of the barracks. "It's too cold to bank the fires, you know, keep 'em simmering all night ready to take off in the morning," Alabama explained. "We usually stoke 'em up again at 4 a.m. so guys wake up toasty and warm. Men who wake up cold get right mean! Tonight we have to just keep the stoves roaring all night. Now don't you tell that you've come into the cave with me—I'm supposed to let you be along but not do! Military regulations!" Alabama smiled and handed Will a poker.

Frost formed on Will's nostrils, his fingers felt like icicles, and his breath, visible in the chill air, was coming in short spurts. Alabama staggered out of the cave with a pile of wood in the wheelbarrow, his now muscular young body working at its peak strength. "Hey Will, I left my tongs in there—I need to go get 'em."

"I'll get 'em, Alabama, just keep going." Will couldn't run; his tired legs and the newly fallen snow made him slow and awkward. Where were the tongs? In the pitch dark of the wood cave entrance he looked for the glint of metal. How far in were they? Would he fall against the side and make the whole mountain of logs fall down on him? If he did, they'd never let him come up to the camp at Ascutney again, and Alabama would get in trouble. His hand hit something—the handles of the tongs! He grabbed the tongs and turned slowly, seeing the snow through the cave door. If the snow had let him he could have tiptoed out of here. He heard a sort of screeching that echoed around him as he reached the door. Going as fast as he could he inched toward Alabama, who was making his slow way to the first of the barracks.

"You okay, Will?" panted Alabama, still clutching the wheelbarrow handles.

"I think that wood mountain's going to cave in!"

They both stopped and listened, hearing a distant howling. "That would be a coyote, kid. A couple of 'em, judging by the sound. I'm hoping that pile is froze so tight that it won't fall—we have four more trips to make. Barracks, then the library, then the state garage. . . ."

What a night! At least the wood mountain never

fell. Time for sleep! As he headed for the barracks, Will could almost feel the hard bunk mattress, as if it were a fluffy feather bed, under his tired body.

As he opened the door, he saw something flicker, a light caught by the corner of his eye. Almost too tired to turn his head, he more felt than saw the flickering grow.

Fully awake now, Will wheeled around to see the flame dancing in the small window of the nearest barracks. He leapt across the frozen walkway between the two buildings and hurled open the door. How could this not have been noticed? Licking flames were tumbling from the open door of the stove.

Will yelled "Fire! Fire!" as he scrambled from his jacket and used it to beat at the flames, now spreading across the pine floor. Skinny figures in long johns surged forward, sleepiness gone in the flying of blankets and splashing of almost frozen water from the pail. Smoke rose.

Alabama, who had gone around to the other side of his barracks to put away the tools, appeared at the door. "What . . . tarnation!" He grabbed a nearby broom and started beating at the few remaining flames.

Soon there was nothing but rising smoke and the

smell of charred wood. Cheers rose up and someone shouted, "Will saved it and us. Burst in here screaming!"

"Somebody get him covered up," someone else said. Will was wrapped in a blanket and hauled up onto shoulders which carried him around the room. Cheers all around!

Calm descended when the barracks captain arrived on the scene, took it all in and said, "So get this young fellow into a warm bed, he'll catch pneumony up there!"

Will, truly in shock, was wrapped in more blankets and carried to Alabama's barracks and deposited, none too gently, onto the bunk amid renewed cheers. The whole camp was awake by this time, as Alabama helped Will unwrap and crawl under the same blankets.

"Do you think we left that stove open?" Will whispered as he drifted off to sleep.

"No!" said Alabama. "That wasn't on our list. We didn't even stoke that stove. There's some mystery here, and I imagine investigating is going to occur, oh is it going to occur! Now don't you worry about explaining why you were out there—a fellow has to go the latrine—and you had permission to be here overnight. . . ."

But Will was sound asleep by then. "Hey buddy, you saved us all!" Alabama whispered as he crawled into his own bunk, also half asleep. "My lucky day when I met up with you, on two counts now! Reading and fire prevention. Hot diggety dog!"

By 8 a.m., when it was time to appear at breakfast, Will had trouble remembering where he was. Then it all came back to him and if that weren't enough, the backslapping and congratulations and general talk around the breakfast table would have reminded him. He was no hero! He shouldn't even have been out there—well, he guessed it was pretty fortunate he was. Right now he was so tired he barely stayed awake through breakfast, so tired he almost wasn't hungry. Almost! He went back to Alabama's barracks and slept until the noon meal. Now he was ravenous!

The snow had stopped when the temperatures dropped so low, and now everything was white, frozen, and still.

"Hey Will!" It was Tom Olsen. Minimal work on the road went on even in the coldest of weather, and he was rounding up the road crew. "I hear tell how you saved all our lives last night."

"Hello, Mr. Olsen. Nah, just lucky to see it, somebody else would've if I hadn't."

"But nobody else did, Will. I guess all the foofaraw is kind of embarrassing, but I personally want to thank you and tell you it makes me proud to have you be one of us."

One of us! Will's mouth fell open, despite the cold. Now, that was an awfully nice thing to hear! "Oh, thank you, Mr. Olsen," he stammered. "I mean, well I mean—that just means an awful lot to me."

Tom Olsen smiled. "Some night duty, huh?"

"Yes sir!" Will hoped Alabama hadn't gotten into trouble by letting him help. Tom Olsen seemed to know all about it.

"Seems the phones were down. Your folks, well, the Mansfields and Jamie, must figure you stayed here, but you better skedaddle on home now."

"Oh, yes! Oh, I wouldn't want them to worry. Thank you, sir!" Will ran back to the barracks and grabbed his snowshoes. He saw Alabama across the mess hall, getting ready to go to firefighting training—well, he'd had some of that last night, for sure. They waved at each other, grinning. Will wanted to thank him, but that could come another time. He strapped on the snowshoes.

What a wonderful year this had been, a whole new life on the mountain, a whole new life in his LIFE! Pretty soon it would be 1934—what adventures would happen then?

View from
Ascutney

Panorama
from the top

Hazy
sunshine

View through
the trees

Winter work

About the Civilian Conservation Corps

The Civilian Conservation Corps was the brainchild of President Franklin Delano Roosevelt. His election as United States president in 1932 came at the height of the Great Depression. The economy was in chaos, unemployment was widespread, and desperation had hit the populace. Families all over the country could barely feed their children, and young men who ordinarily would have been beginning their work life in a trade or occupation were unable to find work or self-respect.

President Roosevelt came up with a plan to put these young unemployed men to work. Eroding soil and declining trees in the country's forests were leading to the destruction of our natural resources. These young men would be employed to renew the nation's forests. Initially called the Emergency Conservation Work Act (ECW), Roosevelt's plan became known as the Civilian Conservation Corps, literally a peacetime army composed of thousands of formerly unemployed young men.

On March 9, 1933, President Roosevelt called the 73rd Congress into emergency session to hear and ratify his program. The legislation was passed on March 31. Granted emergency powers, Roosevelt pledged to have 250,000 men in camps all over the country by the end of July. Before this vastly popular program ended in 1942, over three million young men had planted three billion trees, built roads and trails, shored up dams, created lakes, and constructed stone buildings in both state and national parks and forests nationwide.

From their $30 a month pay, $25 was sent home to their families, in dire need of financial help. The young men became strong and healthy. They were taught to read — in some cases for the first time — and some received high school diplomas from the educational component of the camps. They learned trades and discipline that they carried with them all their lives.

The Civilian Conservation Corps in Vermont employed more than 40,000 men, including 11,243 Vermonters, from 1933 until the advent of World War II. All of Vermont's parks owe their basic visitor structures and the health of their forest lands to the CCC.

Ascutney and Will Ryan: A Note from the Author

I live in a county that has, from many vantage points, a view of the big stone mountain called Ascutney. Officially Mount Ascutney; to those of us who gaze at it and climb it, just Ascutney. And sometimes, just the Mountain: "Think I'll climb the Mountain today. Meet me on the falls trailhead at. . . ." None of the four trails on Ascutney is easy, and I like to take my time getting to the summit, which affords a truly awesome view across and around the Connecticut River valley. A few years ago I volunteered to be a trailhead maintainer and unofficial guide, and I began to learn more about the Mountain and its history. What jumps out at the visitor to Ascutney and all the Vermont state parks are the roads, stone buildings, and campsites, dating back to the 1930s and the Civilian Conservation Corps.

Mount Ascutney is just one small state park that thrived because of the CCC. It is the one I know, and, being a writer, I think of stories to be told. I imagined a young boy, who, like me, thinks of Ascutney as his very own. What would it be like for him to share work and adventures with the only slightly older boys and men of the CCC?

Will Ryan, who lived in West Windsor, Vermont, when it was still mainly a dairy farming community, is totally my own creation, as is his story. The specific corpsmen who are his friends are also imaginary — but their tasks, travails, and stories come from actual details and anecdotes from Ascutney and other camps.

This book covers the first year of the CCC at Ascutney, 1933. This is the first in a series of three books about Will and the corps and their adventures and accomplishments. The next book is set in 1934, and the third in 1935–1936, each of the years the corps was at Ascutney.

About the Photographs

The historic photographs in the book are here thanks to the generous loan of a photo album from Camp #129 on Ascutney Mountain. The album belonged to John Randolph McEachern, a nineteen-year-old CCC member originally from North Quincy, Massachusetts. His only daughter, Sharlene Marie McEachern, loaned them to us for use in all three books of the series.

The photos are from McEachern's collection taken during the years CCC Co. #129 was in residence on Ascutney Mountain. McEachern arrived in 1935; he was from a family of five children who were going through a very hard time during the Great Depression. Like all the young men, he sent home $25 of his $30 a month pay to his family. The men from the camp did find time for some fun, and once in a while they attended dances at the Roseland Ballroom in Claremont, New Hampshire. It was there McEachern met his wife, Rita Bernard. They settled in Windsor, Vermont, where he was a machinist at Cone Blanchard Machine Company. He worked at Cone for forty years, passing away in 1980, at age 64.

According to Sharlene, what her father remembered most about those years on Ascutney, along with good friends who also stayed in Vermont after the camps closed, is how cold it was in rubber boots! Sharlene raised five children in Windsor, and now lives in Brownsville in a historic house, managing properties all over New England. Thank you, Sharlene, for trusting us with these valuable photographic records!

Acknowledgments

I wish to thank Rick White and Ethan Phelps of the State of Vermont Department of Forests, Parks and Recreation for their invaluable help in supplying research materials and thoroughly fact-checking the book. I'd also like to thank Rick for his presentation on the Ascutney CCC camp, which inspired me to write this book, and for connecting me with Sharlene McEachern, who supplied, from her father's photo album, the pictures of the CCC during its years on Ascutney. Thanks also to my good-natured editor, Sarah Novak, who tried to teach me electronic editing and may yet succeed; Ron Toelke, the excellent and thorough designer of the book; Richard CoFrancesco, who slogged through snow to take the cover photo; my grandson Will Varble who slogged with him as "Will Ryan"; the Springfield Library, which put up with my tardy book returns until I finally found an affordable copy of Perry Merrill's *Roosevelt's Forest Army*; Paul Cooper, for helping me design the flier announcing the book and upcoming presentations; and last but not least Tordis Ilg Isselhardt, the wonderful, focused publisher who believed in the book. Plus all the people who knew bits and pieces of the CCC years and with whom I've had brief conversations over several years, among them Jeff Pelton, Barbara Road, Anita Boudelier, Hugh Putnam and . . . I hope I haven't missed anyone! Thank you all!

Judith Edwards
Springfield, Vermont

The Civilian Conservation Corps and Mount Ascutney, Vermont

Book One
INVASION ON THE MOUNTAIN
The Adventures of Will Ryan and the Civilian Conservation Corps, 1933

Book Two
ROAD ON THE MOUNTAIN
The Adventures of Will Ryan and the Civilian Conservation Corps, 1934

Book Three
MOUNTAIN AT THE TOP
The Adventures of Will Ryan and the Civilian Conservation Corps, 1935–36

For Further Exploration

Books

Roosevelt's Forest Army: A History of the Civilian Conservation Corps, 1933- 1942, by Perry H. Merrill. Barre, Vermont: Northlight Studio Press Inc., 1981. (Out of print; available from libraries and online book sites.)

Into the Mountain: Stories of New England's Most Celebrated Peaks, by Maggie Stier and Ron McAdow. Boston, Massachusetts: Appalachian Mountain Club Books, 1995.

The 191st Company, The Civilian Conservation Corps: April 1939–April 1940, by George Galo. Rutland, Vermont: Prime Offset Printing, 1997.

Mount Ascutney Guide, by the Ascutney Trails Association.

Websites

Vermont State Parks home page
   http://www.vtstateparks.com/

Vermont State Parks: Mount Ascutney State Park
   http://www.vtstateparks.com/htm/ascutney.htm

Vermont State Parks and the Civilian Conservation Corps
   http://www.vtstateparks.com/htm/ccc.htm

Ascutney Trails Association
   http://www.ascutneytrails.org/

Civilian Conservation Corps Legacy
   http://www.ccclegacy.org

Topics and Questions for Discussion

1. Will, in 1933, lives on a farm with his aunt and uncle. He does lots of farm chores. Sometimes doing those chores means he can't go to school.
How is that different from your life today? Why, at Will's farm, do chores come before school?

2. Despite being needed on the farm and missing a lot of school because of the chores, Will very much likes to learn. Will has a teacher he likes, and who teaches Will whenever he can.
What are your thoughts about this, as a modern-day student?

3. At first Will is upset that his special friend and place of safety, Ascutney Mountain, will be invaded. Then he gets excited about how he can be of help. He makes friends, on and off the mountain.
What do you think about this? How does this make you feel about Will's chances of being a happy person, despite the meanness of his Uncle Em?

4. The millions of young men of the Civilian Conservation Corps signed up because times were hard, their families were poor, and they had few education or job prospects.

Do you think if your circumstances were similar, you could work as hard as they did, and follow all those rules? If not, why not?

5. The legislation that created the Civilian Conservation Corps came about during a terrible crisis for the United States.
What do you know about the New Deal, the daring programs instituted by President Franklin Roosevelt to help his country survive this economic catastrophe?

6. Do you like mountains? The Civilian Conservation Corps worked on many mountains in the United States. If you have visited a state or national park, you probably have walked on a road or stayed near a camp built by the CCC.
Research the work the CCC has accomplished for our parks, either in one state or around the country.

7. Will discovers many things during this story. One is that he has learned a lot of practical skills on the farm, despite Uncle Em's harshness. He also discovers that he likes to help out, and that he isn't as shy as he thought.
When Will has overcome many of the obstacles to his learning, and he can visit Ascutney as often as he likes, how do you imagine his life will change?

8. Jamie Maken, the farmer, and Sam Mansfield, Will's teacher, as well as CCC foreman Tom Olsen, are kind and caring people who are very helpful to Will.
Who in your own life has influenced you to become your best self?

About the Author

Judith Edwards lives and writes in an old farmhouse near Mount Ascutney State Park. Ascutney looms over the area and is a favorite hiking and camping site, full of history. It is not as tall as the Rocky Mountains that formed the backdrop for her three books on the  Lewis and Clark Expedition (that "magnificent geographical unfolding") nor as rugged. However, Ascutney's development by the Civilian Conservation Corps in the 1930s was her inspiration to write yet another book of history for young people.

Originally from Colorado where snow and mountains to hike are always near, she has traveled widely, first as a performer/director/teacher, then doing research on her special love, history. Judith is the author of twelve books for children's, middle grade, and young adult audiences, and has written numerous articles for New England publications such as *Vermont Life, Down East,* and *Yankee* magazines. Her performing background comes in handy as she presents programs based on her books' historical subjects to schools and libraries all over the Northeast.

Currently she is hard at work on the second book in the Will Ryan and the CCC series, and, like Will, can't wait until spring to once again climb her "own" mountain, Ascutney.

Books by Judith Edwards

Colter's Run

Lewis and Clark's Journey of Discovery

The Lindbergh Baby Kidnapping

Nat Turner's Rebellion

Jamestown, John Smith and Pocahontas

The Plymouth Colony and the Pilgrim Adventure

Henry Hudson and his Voyages of Discovery

Lenin and the Russian Revolution

Abolitionists and Slave Resistance

The History of the American Indians and the Reservation

Bending Moments: Crossing the Uncomfort Zone To Change

For more information about Judith Edwards
and her writing and presentations, visit:
http://judithedwards.com/